THIS BOOK BELONG TO

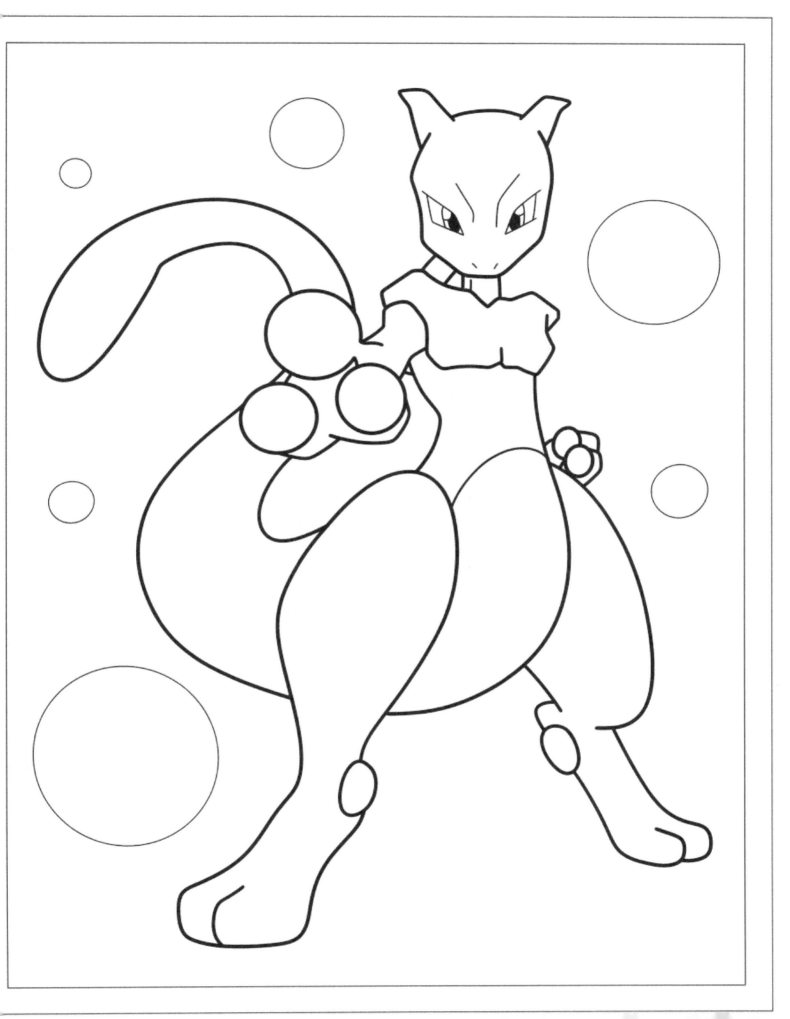

Basic Pokémon
Mewtwo
60 HP

Genetic Pokémon. Length: 6' 7", Weight: 269 lbs.

 Psychic Does 10 damage plus 10 more damage for each Energy card attached to the Defending Pokémon. **10+**

 Barrier Discard 1 ⊙ Energy card attached to Mewtwo in order to prevent all effects of attacks, includeing damage, done to Mewtwo during your opponent's next turn.

weakness	resistance	retreat cost

A scientist created this Pokémon after years of horrific gene-splicing and DNA engineering experiments. LV. 53   #150

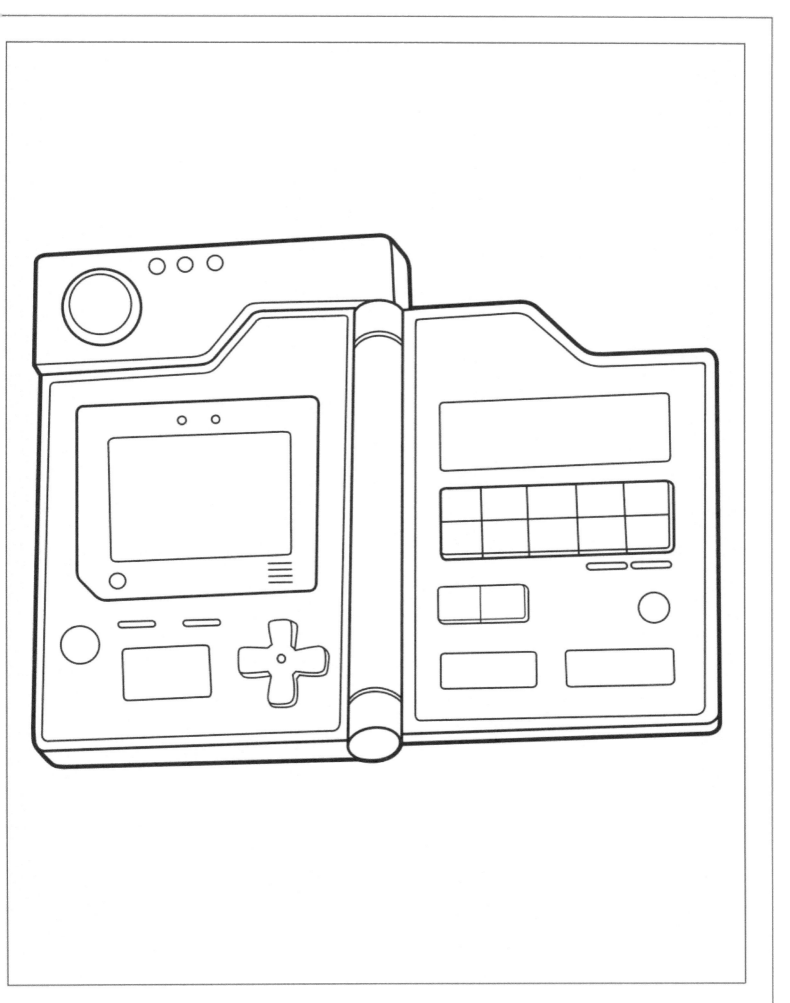

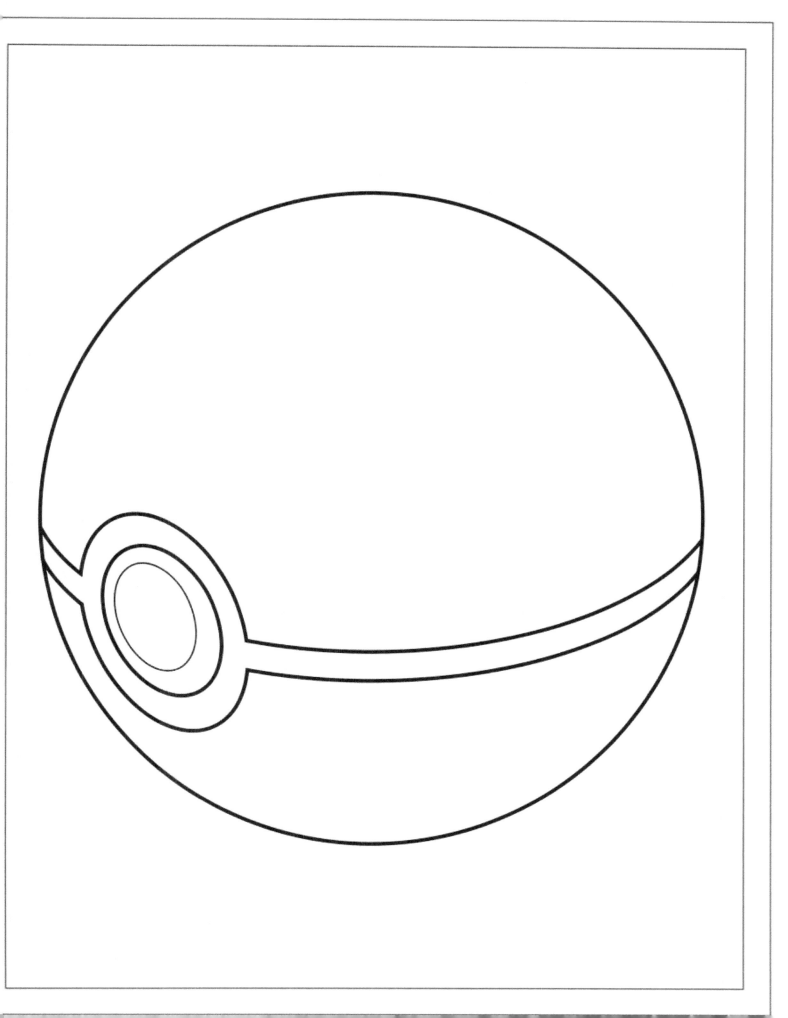

Stage 2 — Evolves from Wartortle — Put Blastoise on the Stage 1 card

Venusaur   100 HP

Seed Pokémon. Length: 6' 7", Weight: 220.5 lbs.

Pokémon Power: Energy Trans As often as you like during your turn, you may move a ⊛ Energy from 1 of your Pokémon to another of your Pokémon. This Pokémon Power can't be used if this Pokémon is Asleep, Confused, or Paralyzed.

Solar Beam   60

weakness   resistance   retreat cost

This plant blooms when it is absorbing solar enrgy. It stays on the move to seek sunlight.   LV. 67   #3

Printed in the USA
CPSIA information can be obtained
at www.ICGtesting.com
CBHW080354140824
13133CB00027B/783